HAMBLE

Images of the past 150 years from the village scrapbook

Audrey Monk & Gabrielle Mabley

Design & Artwork by Joolz Williams

Gaymonk Books

First published in Great Britain 2000
by Gaymonk Books

Design and Artwork by Joolz Williams

Published by Gaymonk Books

Printed by Intype London Ltd.
Units 3/4, Elm Grove Industrial Estate
Elm Grove, Wimbledon
London SW19 4HE

ISBN No.: 0 9539632 0 9 - *Images of Hambledon*

Front Cover Illustration: *Haymaking c. 1900*

Back Cover Illustrations: *Mervil Hill*
                              Malthouse Farm
                              Philpots

Acknowledgments

The authors gratefully acknowledge the encouragement and support of many people, but especially Muriel Campbell, Mary Caröe, Stephen Dean, Joan Hardy, Ron Head, George Pitt, Stuart Cook, David Williams and Jane Woolley, whose comments and help have been much appreciated.

The authors also thank sincerely the Hambledon Heritage Society and Hambledon Parish Council for permission to use material from the Village Scrapbook, Domestic Buildings Research Group, the Surrey Advertiser and Annabel Watts for permission to use their illustrations and photographs.

We are also grateful to Mary Caröe, Stephen Dean, David Pitt, David Williams, Michael Worsfold and Jane Woolley for the use of photographs from their private collections.

The authors apologise for the omission of any persons whom they may have inadvertently not acknowledged.

Foreword

All Hambledonians owe a great debt of gratitude to Audrey Monk and Gabrielle Mabley for researching and collating this delightful book which will be enjoyed and treasured by us all.

The Scrapbook from which the material is drawn was originally made by my mother, Betty Wieler. Later my aunt, Mary Parker, had it rebound by Antony Gardener, a well-known local bookbinder. Mary Parker also wrote her own Memories of Hambledon and The History of the Church.

In 1999 sufficient funds were collected by Hambledonians to professionally conserve the original Scrapbook at a cost of £3,548.50 in memory of Mary Parker. The original is housed in Godalming Museum and a loan copy is kept at the Village Shop.

Subsequent scrapbooks have been made and maintained by Joan Hardy. A small group is keeping the history up to date.

I was born in Hambledon and have loved it all my life. Everyone here can feel part of an extended family whose joys and griefs are shared, and this spirit persists making it one of the best places in which to live.

My hope is that future generations will continue to be interested in the past and enjoy living in Hambledon in such a way that its pleasant atmosphere is cherished.

Muriel Campbell

June 2000

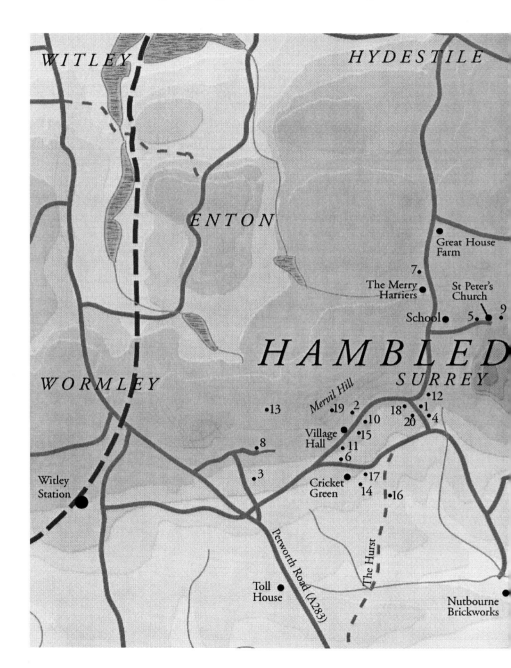

WITLEY

HYDESTILE

ENTON

Great House
Farm

7.

The Merry
Harriers •

St Peter's
Church

School•   5.• •9

HAMBLED

WORMLEY

SURREY

Mervil Hill

•12

•13   •19 •2   18• •1
                                •4
              •10   20
Village •   •1
Hall   •15
         •11
•8   •6

•3   •17
        Cricket •
        Green   14 •16

Witley
Station

The Hurst

Toll
House

Petworth Road (A283)

Nutbourne
Brickworks

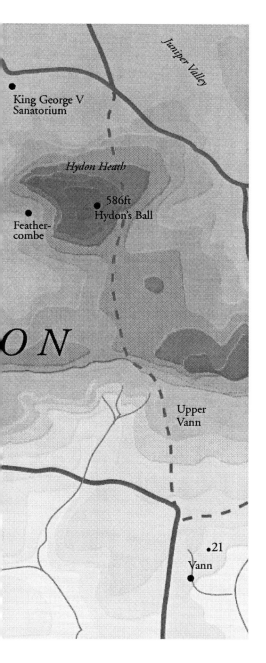

King George V
Sanatorium

Juniper Valley

Hydon Heath

586ft
Hydon's Ball

Feather-
combe

O N

Upper
Vann

•21

Vann

Key

1 Almshouses, old (site of)
2 Almshouses, new
3 Cherryhurst
4 Cobblers (cottage)
5 Court Farm
6 Cricket Green Stores
7 Glebe House
8 Hambledon Homes
9 Lime Kiln
10 Malthouse
11 Mann's Cottage (site of)
12 Matteryes (site of)
13 Moor Cottage
14 Oakhurst Cottage
15 Paddock Close
16 Philpots
17 Rose Cottage
18 Shipton Hill
19 St. Dominic's
20 Upper Green
21 Vann Copse Glassworks (site of)

Images of Hambledon

During the 1950s and 1960s members of the Women's Institute collected together photographs and memorabilia about Hambledon dating back to the mid-nineteenth century and compiled the Village Scrapbook.

Using material from the Scrapbook, this portrayal of the village looks back over the past 150 years and attempts to draw together some of the stories behind the photos and to reflect the changes that time and social circumstances have made.

The end of the twentieth century saw the population increase with the building of two estates at opposite ends of the village: Hambledon Park and The Hydons. Houses in the village change hands fairly frequently and, although people born and bred in Hambledon are fewer and fewer, some families can trace their ancestry through the church registers for several centuries.

The Village Hall, the Village Green, the Nursery School, the Church, and the Pub, continue to play a central role. To outsiders, Hambledon may perhaps seem very quiet but those who live here know what a huge variety of interests and activities take place, renewing and enhancing its sense of community.

Unlike earlier centuries, most people now work away from the village, travelling many miles by car or train. The last remaining big employers have moved elsewhere but, in contrast, a few small workshops have opened offering a variety of services. Witley and Milford railway stations are too far to reach without transport. Most households own at least one car and many families have bicycles. A familiar sight on both the roads and the bridleways are the horses which are kept for pleasure riding.

The village was very different in earlier centuries. By far the most noticeable difference is that at the end of the nineteenth century and for the first half of the twentieth century there were several shops, including a baker, a grocer, a butcher, a saddler, a sweet shop and a cobbler - and the village was almost self-sufficient [1].

Apart from the cobbler, all these individual shops had gone by the 1960s, only the one general store and post office replacing them, now called Cricket Green Stores.

Since the nineteenth century (with the exception of 1991) there has always been a post office, though moving from cottage to cottage over the years.

Shipton Hill Post Office from 1855-1893

When the general store and post office, which had flourished for years, closed suddenly in 1990 it was realised that the village had lost a great treasure. However, as happened in times past, some very energetic people got together, formed a committee and with much help and hard work from many villagers managed to open the shop and post office again in 1992[2]. This time it was a community shop in every sense of the word. The only paid person is the Manager and all the other helpers are unpaid volunteers. It is still running successfully and no one would want to be without it.

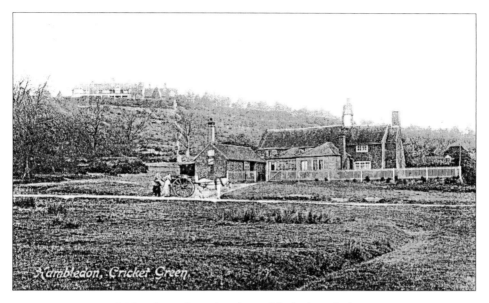

Cricket Green Stores has changed little through the ages
Below left: 1909   Below: c.1965   Above: c.1900

Hambledon is mentioned in the Domesday Survey of 1086 taxed for three hides, perhaps some 300 acres. Earlier, in the time of King Edward, it was taxed for five hides. The exact location of Hambledon in the early Middle Ages is not known. The Survey refers to a mill, but the site is now lost; no church is mentioned[3].

The present Church of St. Peter was built by the Reverend Edward Bullock in 1846, substantially replacing an earlier church believed to date from *c.* 1100[4].

The Church

Sadly, the Norman font was removed at the time of the re-building. It was purchased in 1848 by the architect, Mr. Woodyer, when refurbishing St. Martha's Church, Chilworth, where it can now be seen.

The first recorded Incumbent is Robert, described as Parson of Hambledon, in 1278[5].

The Font

A description[6] of the old Church in 1824 describes it as being built with rough materials, covered partly with tiles and partly with stone slates, with a brick floor, and a gallery on the north and at the west end. There was a small open chapel on the north belonging to the manor. The wooden turret housed one bell, surmounted by a shingle-covered spire.

In the Churchyard are two magnificent yew trees, one of which has a girth of 32 feet (10m) and is completely hollow. When measured in 1905 by E.W. Swanton, Curator of Haslemere Museum, it was 28 feet 6 inches (8.69 m)[7] and Mary Parker records that a school teacher once told her that when she had taken her class of infants up to the Churchyard, all 33 infants had clambered in together[8].

The older tree is said to be of great age, some say 2,000 years, but still in good heart and one of the finest three or four in England[9].

Many parishes wished to mark the millennium by planting yew trees and in 1996 cuttings were taken from the Hambledon yew to be planted elsewhere. During the millennium year a further 300-400 cuttings were taken[10].

The Old Yew

During the nineteenth century, one of the more important buildings in the village was the school, built in 1852. It was a National School (run by the Church) but it was not until the Education Act of 1870 that it became compulsory to send children to school. The original buildings were small and were enlarged in 1874 and 1962[11]. The first remaining school log book (1884-1890) reveals a very different way of life[12]. Some children had to walk many miles to school and consequently when there was bad weather many children did not come at all.

During harvesting many children were away picking hops, whortleberries, acorns and chestnuts and helping with the harvest.

The Rector, his wife and daughters and other ladies took a great interest and frequently visited the school, sometimes to teach, sometimes to examine, and sometimes to give prizes and leaving certificates.

Left: Girls' Spinning Class
Below: Hambledon School Pupils in 1865

Her Majesty's Inspectors came once a year and, year after year, they complained about the general dilapidation of the buildings and the lack of books and equipment for the children.

The children were taught by a Mistress, a pupil teacher and a monitress who was chosen from the top class, the number of pupils varying from none (due to bad weather) to 104.

When they left school at the age of 12, the boys went to work on the farms or at a trade, the girls mostly went into service, though some became pupil teachers and were able to better themselves.

The school was also used as a "Village Hall" with Night Classes for the men and, once a year, for the distribution of Smith's Charity[13]. A piano was installed for "Parochial Entertainment" and there were Penny Readings in the evening. The school continued to be the focal point for the education of children of Hambledon until 1983 when it was closed by Surrey County Council[14].

Below: The Village School   Above: Schoolboy Gardeners

Above: Pupils in 1983, shortly before the school closed
Top left: Pupils in 1895
Bottom left: Pupils in 1949

Soon after the school closed, a group of people from the village joined together to buy the buildings and start a Nursery School. They found the building was leaking and had no furniture or fittings. After much renovation it was opened for mornings only, three times a week and became a charitable trust[(15)].

It was soon possible to increase the numbers to seventy pupils and the school opened five mornings and four afternoons a week. It continues to flourish and to educate the younger children of the village and surrounding areas.

The Almshouses too have played an important part in the life of the village. Their origin is obscure but they existed in 1767. It is believed that the cottages, painted by Birket Foster between 1860 and 1864, were the old almshouses. Because the painting was sold for one hundred guineas, the lane (which used to be called Sandhole Lane) became known thereafter as Hundred Guinea Lane[16].

Painting by Myles Birket Foster entitled 'Cottage at Hambledon'

There is no record of a transfer of the land on which the Almshouses were built, but in 1865 they were described as built of brick with thatched roofs "now so dilapidated as to be hardly fit for occupation" and there were plans to pull them down[17]. This proposal fell through; the almshouses remained and in 1867 public subscription raised money to repair them. A great tragedy is reputed to have occurred there one night: Mr. Boxall, who lived in one at the far end where there was a big drop, fell into the lane and was killed[18].

In 1890 the almshouses were condemned by the Statutory Authorities and in 1891 a Committee was formed with the purpose of building new almshouses. A site was found in Malthouse Lane but efforts to raise sufficient funds, again by public subscription as the almshouses were not endowed, were unsuccessful. The money had to be returned to subscribers, retaining only sufficient to put the almshouses in a proper state of repair.

Almshouses in 1904[19]

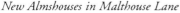

Disaster struck once more in 1904 when the steps and retaining wall collapsed into the Lane. The funding problems were finally resolved and in 1907 the two new almshouses were built in Malthouse Lane, one in memory of John Borrowman and the other of Mary Bonham Carter. The architect was Mr. H. Moon[20].

New Almshouses in Malthouse Lane

Visitations by the Bishops of Winchester in the eighteenth century are very dismissive of the Parish: the number of souls "may reasonably be supposed to be about 200", but "there is not one nobleman, gentleman or person of note of either sex in the parish". Some sixty years later the number was put at 399[21]. Early nineteenth century records show that the number of inhabitants was remarkably about the same[22]. The economy of the village was entirely agricultural and had probably changed little.

Lane outside Malthouse Farm

Another important institution during the nineteenth century was the Hambledon Workhouse, built in 1786, initially to serve the parishes of Hambledon, Dunsfold, Chiddingfold and Bramley. The impact on the village must have been tremendous, increasing the number of inhabitants by some 150. By the end of the nineteenth century it had the reputation of being one of the happiest and best organised of its kind. This was due in no small part to the Board of Governors and local gentry who took a great interest in the welfare of its residents[23].

In 1930 Surrey County Council took over the running of the Workhouse and built additional accommodation, which became known as Hambledon Homes. During the Second World War the inmates were evacuated and the premises used by King Edward's School, Wormley, as their buildings had been taken over by the Admiralty. After the war, the School returned to its old site.

The Hambledon Homes

During the 1970s the Homes were closed and the site sold to the Institute of Oceanographic Sciences. When they moved to Southampton in 1995, the site was sold for development and became Hambledon Park. The workhouse buildings were retained as flats and executive houses were built in the grounds. A plaque, rescued from the workhouse buildings, is now displayed adjacent to the public footpath through the estate.

Plaque from the original building

This House was Erected by the United Parishes of Bramley Chiddingfold, Dunsfold and Hambledon for the better Relief and Employment of the Poor. Anno Domini 1786

For hundreds of years, for most people, walking was the only way of getting around unless you were rich enough to own a horse or could obtain a lift from the carter. Roads were bad and the main road between Godalming and Petworth, which ran through Hambledon Hurst, was particularly notorious.

Road through The Hurst

Queen Anne's husband, Prince George of Denmark, travelling from Windsor to Petworth, took fourteen hours and the coach stuck and had to be man-handled through the worst patches of Hambledon clay. It took them six hours to travel the last nine miles[24].

Improvements were made and from 1750 onwards turnpike roads were built, the local one being from Witley, over Culmer and Wormley Hill and on to Chiddingfold (the A283). These were toll roads and toll cottages were built to take the revenue.

The Toll House

Change came with the railway when the line was extended from Godalming to Haslemere in 1859[25]. In 1898 a local philanthropist gave land to build a new road from Lane End to Witley Station "to save the horses the steep climb up Wormley Hill"[26].

Witley Station

By the early twentieth century, cars, buses and charabancs had become more common, though Harold Hutchins remembered that as small boys he and his friends would wait at Lane End to write down car numbers and were lucky if they saw more than twelve cars in a day[27].

The Surrey Hills proved a great attraction for artists and writers of the day who, venturing forth from the suburbs of London, found to their delight a countryside and landscape largely untouched.

Myles Birket Foster (1825-1899) moved into the area from St. John's Wood in about 1862. He lived at Tigbourne Cottage, at the bottom of Lane End, before buying land at the top of Wormley Hill where, in 1864, he built The Hill largely to his own design[28].

George Eliot purchased The Heights and Helen Allingham lived at Sandhills. The area had great charm for Birket Foster and Helen Allingham, both of whom painted widely in Witley, Chiddingfold and Hambledon[29]

Malthouse Farm by Helen Allingham

Matteryes (demolished 1965) was one of the larger houses built at this time. It used to stand on the bank facing the well by Woodlands Road and once reached fame by being featured in *The Traveller* of 22 June 1901 following an adventure concerning two balloonists:

> *"By a remarkable coincidence, some while later one of the balloonists was travelling from London to Portsmouth by train and, as they travelled through Witley, regaled his companion with the story of the 'near miss' and how they had badly scared the two old gentlemen playing croquet on the lawn At this point a quiet man in the corner of the carriage remarked "Well I was one of the two old gentlemen ... I was afraid you were going to fly off with my house".*

THE TRAVELLER

[June 22, 1901]

" LOOK OUT THERE, OR YOU'LL HOOK ON TO MY CHIMNEY POTS."

Mervil Hill, now St. Dominic's School, was built in the late nineteenth century and was at one time the home of John Franklin-Adams who, according to Mary Parker, was the first person in the village to own a motor car. Mr Franklin-Adams was an astronomer of some repute. He moved to Mervil Hill in 1904 and built an observatory, from which he commenced the immense task of making a photographic chart of the heavens over the northern hemisphere[30].

During the First World War it was a convalescent home, as much fresh air was considered essential for a speedy return to good health.

"An hour's rest" on the terrace, St. Dominic's Open-air School, "Mount Olivet"

St Dominic's School

Above: An hour's rest on the terrace

Left: The Chapel

Mervil Hill then became the home of Mrs. Weguelin who, after the death of her husband, handed over her country residence to the Sisters of the Sacred Hearts of Jesus and Mary for use as a residential school for delicate boys. So, in 1929, St. Dominic's was founded.

Now the school admits girls as well as boys and has a growing reputation for excellence, catering for children with special needs, both physical and emotional.

St Dominic's School
Right: The Gardens
Below: Junior Class

In 1906 the Great House Estate was auctioned together with "an exceptionally beautiful site" with quarries of blue bargate and of ironstone nearby to facilitate the building of a residence[31].

It was on this site that Eric Parker, naturalist and author of several books on the Surrey landscape, built Feathercombe in 1910.

The name of the house was taken from the field named "The Fethercooms"[32].

The house, designed by architect Ernest Newton, did not make use of the local quarries but was built of brown brick with red brick dressings[33]. The bargate stone was, however, used by Eric Parker in his design for the beautiful garden round the house[34].

Eric Parker

Feathercombe

Glebe House dates from the seventeenth century and was refronted in 1710 during the incumbency of the Reverend Joseph Richardson. It was the Rectory until 1930, when a smaller modern house was built on part of the glebe land. Glebe House was then acquired by the Misses Allfrey who lived in the house until 1954.

Glebe House, originally the old Rectory, painted by V.M. Allfrey

Vann

Vann is one of the oldest houses still standing in the village and was originally an open-hall house dating from about 1540[35]. Successive owners have added to the house: in 1689 it was acquired by John Childe, three times Mayor of Guildford. In 1907 W.D. CarÖe came to Vann and re-modelled the house for his own use, and it has been the home of the CarÖe family ever since.

The Water Garden was designed by Gertrude Jekyll in 1911[36].

Water Garden at Vann

The name Vann means marshy place and dates back to the twelfth century. It was not then in the parish of Hambledon but was a tithing of Godalming, and records of tenants and tithingmen at Vann occur often in the Godalming Hundred Court[37].

But it was the smaller houses that attracted the attention of the artists and writers.

Oakhurst Cottage by Helen Allingham

Oakhurst Cottage, also painted by Birket Foster, was originally a sixteenth-century barn. It became a dwelling in the seventeenth century and was inhabited until 1981. In the early twentieth century it was acquired, with other lands in Hambledon, by James Joicey who purchased The Hill on Wormley Hill (the home of Birket Foster). Sadly, Mr. Joicey met with severe financial problems, the estate passed to his wife and was subsequently sold. Cottages in Hambledon were purchased by the Allfrey sisters, who lived at Glebe House, and Mrs. Ruth Parker (wife of Eric Parker), who lived at Feathercombe, to enable the tenants to remain living in them.

Oakhurst, one of the cottages acquired, is now owned by the National Trust and open, by appointment, to the public during the summer, with local residents acting as stewards. It houses several items from the Gertrude Jekyll Collection.

Interior of Oakhurst Cottage

Gertrude Jekyll lived at Busbridge and moved to Munstead Wood in 1897. In addition to her famed collaboration with Edwin Lutyens, she landscaped over 300 gardens, including those at Great House, Vann and Tigbourne Court.

In her book *Old West Surrey*[38] she tried to capture 'the ways and lives and habitations of the older people' and, lamenting the loss of the 'solid furniture of pure material and excellent design', she made a collection of some items, many of which are housed at Guildford Museum.

Mr. and Mrs. Bookham photographed outside their home near Hydon Ball on the 60th anniversary of their wedding day

A typical scene beloved by Gertrude Jekyll. This is Mrs. Goodchild (bottom right in picture) at her cottage, now called Cobblers, in Sandhole Lane

This well (below) would have been used by Mrs. Goodchild and other cottagers along Sandhole Lane. The well-head still stands and remained in use until the 1950s.

In the eighteenth century, this area was known as Upper Green[39].

The Well

Many of the smaller cottages are timber framed and date from the late sixteenth/seventeenth century.

Rose Cottage is situated on the edge of what is now the Cricket Green. It is here seen decorated for the 1953 Coronation Village Competition in which it won third prize.

Moor Cottage, on Hambledon Common, was originally a three-bay timber-framed cottage. Unusually, it has a floored attic at one end.

Philpots is situated in The Hurst. The 1844 Tithe Award records that Philpots was a smallholding with eight acres of meadowland, valued at £1.8s.6d. (£1.43). Note the large barn, typical of many in the village.

Philpots - the two boys are fishing for eels.

A sketch of 1887 entitled "Edward's Cottage". The cottage is now demolished but was probably near Mervil Bottom.

*Mr. and Mrs. Thomas Hammond who lived on Cricket Green.
Thomas, an agricultural labourer, was born in Hambledon
in 1839 and spent all his life there.*

Malthouse Farm, illustrated earlier in a painting by Helen Allingham, dates back to the seventeenth century. As its name implies it was once a malthouse, an extensive complex used for drying hops. The earliest maltster known at present was William Woods, who died on the 8 July 1836[(40)]. His wife, Maria Woods, was granted Letters of Administration and took over the business. She is recorded in the Tithe Award of 1844 as the maltster.

Hops were grown in the village and picked by school children. Hops can still be found in the hedgerows along Malthouse Lane and elsewhere in the village.

By 1851, however, the Census Returns record the property as a farm in the ownership of Thomas Oliver, comprising some 125 acres. It remained a farm until 1961 and the old dairy still exists[(41)].

Sketch of Malthouse dairy from Report by Domestic Buildings Research Group

Skeffington Hume Dodgson was Curate of Hambledon between 1871 and 1874 and lodged at Malthouse Farm; he was visited there on several occasions by his brother, Charles Lutwidge Dodgson (Lewis Carroll), and his sisters, who lived at Guildford[42].

Among other celebrated visitors to Hambledon were Oscar Wilde and Charles Darwin.

In the late nineteenth century and before the present Village Hall was built, meetings were held in a room at Malthouse Farm.

A Group of Ladies seated outside Malthouse Farm, c. 1900.
Their names are recorded.

Court Farm

Court Farm was one of the larger farms of the Manor reaching up on to Hydon's Ball with its lands lying in the parishes of Hambledon and Godalming. It is not clear whether it was ever the Manor House, but a Deed of 1817 refers to the then Lord of the Manor reserving the right to hold the Court for the Manor in a messuage belonging to Court Farm.

Court Farm Buildings

Great House farm was the largest farm in the village in the second half of the nineteenth century. In 1841 it was farmed by John Woods, described to Gertrude Jekyll by one old woman as *"the quietest and best master I ever lived with. There was the red brick kitchen floor. I used to flow he down with a green broom; best of brooms for bricks; makes the floors red. You makes 'em of the green broom as grows on the common"* (43).

In 1861 the farm, by then some 300 acres, was farmed by Cyrus Ellis.

Mr and Mrs Cyrus Ellis with their family

By 1871 the farm had grown to 485 acres and employed thirteen men and nine boys[44]. Other men in the village would have been employed to do odd jobs as account books of the time show:

15 March 1851 Wm Buss, planting 13,100 chestnut
@ 2/0 a thousand. £1.6s.2¹/₂d

29 March 1851 Rich. Furlonger tying hay 25 loads 8 truss   £1.17s.10d

29 March 1852 H. Boxall making 8 sheep cages @ 7d each   4s.8d

31 December 1852 Eliott two & half days bricklaying at 2s.10d.   7s.3d

Villagers, although poor, were skilled and masters of their craft.

Hoop Shaver[45]

Snookety Bookham, who could neither read nor write, was renowned as a rickmaker

Many farmers built their own kilns to lime the fields, and one can still be seen near the church. It was common practice for the farmers to take lump lime straight from the kiln to the fields and disperse it in small heaps over the field. It would then be covered with earth and left to slake by interaction with water, eventually falling to a powder which was then ploughed in.

Above: Prize animals at Great House

Left: The Lime Kiln near the church

A typical Hambledon Granary, possibly at Great House farm.

Not to be forgotten is The Merry Harriers, no doubt the focus for many a thirsty farm labourer. In 1841 it was known as The Hare & Hound and, earlier still, by the sign of The Wheatsheaf[(46)]. In 1892 the Licensing Returns record that it was a tied house providing accommodation and stabling.

The Merry Harriers

In 1844 employment in the village was largely on the land or "in service". However, although agriculture had probably always been a major source of employment, industry too has played its part.

Medieval glass-works have been excavated at Blundens Wood[47] and at Vann Copse, and the extraction of sand from the Common, which continued over several centuries, did not cease until the 1950s[48].

The old brickworks near the Cricket Green is recorded in documents dating back to the eighteenth century, and it is only recently that Nutbourne Brickworks closed down. The future of the site is not known at present.

Right: Excavations at Vann Copse, 1932
Below: Nutbourne Brickworks

NUTBOURNE BRICKWORKS LTD.,
HAMBLEDON, GODALMING, SURREY.
Telephone Wormley 204

The owners of Nutbourne Brickworks built houses for their workers, and this was one of the first twentieth-century developments. Others included the building of Cherryhurst in 1962.

Cherryhurst

Paddock Close was built after World War II on land compulsorily purchased by Hambledon Rural District Council.

Paddock Close under construction

Opposite Paddock Close is the Village Hall, formerly known as The Institute. The land was given by the Lord and Lady of the Manor, Mr. and Mrs. James Mellersh. Many wealthy people subscribed to the new building and there were many smaller donations from villagers.

The New Hambledon Institute

In the *Haslemere Herald* of 31 October 1903 there is a report of the opening: *"The Institute, which is brick built with a tiled roof, chiefly consists of a large room with a platform at one end. It is intended to partition off this room into two parts by a moving wooden shutter. Adjoining the main room are a reading room and a committee room and, on the other side, there are two spacious lobbies. The cost was £700, all of which money has been raised".*

Since then the Village Hall has been enlarged by the addition of a kitchen and lavatories, and there have been other general improvements. A few years ago the bank was dug out to enlarge the area for parking. The Hall will, yet again, have to be brought up-to-date because of the new EU regulations.

The Scrapbook includes no memories of the First World War, although there is a memorial in the Church. The war of 1939-45 left its mark on Hambledon. On 23 October 1940, a passing German bomber dropped five bombs, one of which hit Mann's Cottage killing three adults and two children. The only survivor was a baby asleep upstairs in a cot which was blown straight up in the air, and descended on to the top of the rubble, with its occupant unharmed[49]. There is a memorial in Hambledon Church.

Mann's Cottage

Bomb damage at Court Farm

The Cottage was so-named as Mr. Mann, the village blacksmith, once lived there, with his smithy next door. The smithy is still there, but has been incorporated into a garage. Heath Cottage has been built on the site of Mann's Cottage. The farm buildings at Court Farm were also bombed, leaving a sea of devastation. Luckily, Court Farm itself escaped.

King George V Sanatorium was built as a Tuberculosis Isolation Hospital in 1922. In the early stages of the war, a wooden-hutted complex was built on land to the east of King George V as an emergency hospital for air-raid casualties and many of the nurses were accommodated in the village. The walk back through the woods from the hospital at night held much terror for those for whom life in the country was a new experience.

Lack of civilian casualties resulted in the hospital being taken over by the Australians for wounded servicemen, who could often be seen wandering around the country-side. When, in 1941, St. Thomas's Hospital was bombed in London, patients and staff were evacuated to the complex, which was greatly expanded[50].

These two hospitals became known as the Hydestile Hospitals, now the site of The Hydons.

Aerial View of Hydestile Hospitals

Hambledon became the home for evacuee children from Battersea[51] and many must have found life very strange. Few houses would have had mains drainage, and some no electricity; a trip to the privy at night must have been terrifying.

The different lifestyles of town and country dwellers, as well as backgrounds, made settling down difficult for many of the evacuees. Some were very homesick but, for others, it was a happy experience and many returned after the war to say so.

Mr. Milligan, who was the village schoolmaster, was also a member of the Home Guard and was said to keep "the armoury" upstairs in the spare bedroom at Reyden Cottage (now Bryony Bank)[52].

Above and below: Evacuees
Left: Sgt. Milligan

Hambledon Church Choir 1910

He was also choir master and a plaque in his memory may be seen in the Church. Mr. Milligan seems to have played a great part in the life of the village.

The choir on their annual outing

May Day was a holiday for the children. A May Queen was chosen and all the girls dressed up with pretty frocks and carried garlands.

May Day 1915 outside Hydon End

Other occasions for celebration were the coronations of King Edward VII in 1902, of King George V in 1911, King George VI in 1937 and Queen Elizabeth II in 1953. The village also celebrated the Silver Jubilee of King George V in 1935, when Mr. Van Gruisen, the Lord of the Manor, planted an oak tree on Upper Green[53].

The Village Hall, the Green, and the Rectory Garden, were the scene of many celebrations.

Children's VE Day party on the green

Coronation celebrations outside the Village Hall

Maypole dancing on the Rectory Lawn in 1949

Cricket, played by both sexes, is dear to the heart of Hambledon and has a long tradition. A press report of 1745 describes "the greatest match ever played in the south of England" when eleven maids of Hambledon defeated eleven maids of Bramley on Gosden Common [54].

In 1884 the Rector commanded that a large number of children absent from school on account of "a grand cricket match in the village" were to be punished [55]. Over the years Hambledonians, young and old, have no doubt seen many closely fought battles.

The four Jeffreys Brothers, one of several local families who featured prominently in the Hambledon team, in 1934

Below: Tie between Hambledon, Surrey and Hambledon, Hampshire in 1937

It was not until 1950 that Mrs.Van Gruisen, then Lady of the Manor, gave the Green in trust to the parish to ensure that the Green would be preserved in perpetuity [56].

The deeds were handed over during an all-day match between Hambledon and Thornton Heath on August Bank Holiday (Hambledon won).

Today the Club boasts a 1st and 2nd Eleven, and a thriving Colts section.

Cricket on the green today. Above: 1st Eleven; Below: Hambledon Colts

In some ways Hambledon, at the beginning of the twenty-first century, seems to have changed little. It is still much loved by its residents and visitors attracted to the surrounding hills, now formally designated an Area of Outstanding Natural Beauty.

A hundred years ago, before the bracken and birch were allowed to grow, the Common was open heathland and grazed by cows.

Drawing of Hambledon from Mervil Hill dated 1838

During the twentieth century, the Common became overgrown with bracken, birch and scrub. Stephen Dean, the son of the present Lord of the Manor, is now returning the common to its former heathland habitat. The Greensand Way crosses the ridge and views to Blackdown and the South Downs have once more been revealed. Woodlarks returned in 1998.

Pride in the village remains constant. Hambledon again won the Best Kept Village Competition in 1999 and, in February 2000 as part of the Millennium celebrations, two oak trees were planted outside the Village Hall by children of the village.

Best Kept village 1999. Ion Campbell, Chairman of Hambledon Parish Council, receiving plaque from Audrey Cooper, Chairman of Surrey Voluntary Services Council

Tree planting for the Millennium February 2000

Footnotes

1 *Memories of Hambledon,* Mary Parker, 1989.
"Besides the village shop, there were at one time a baker, a butcher, a saddler, two sweetshops and four boot repairers."

2 Hambledon Village Shop Committee records.

3 *Domesday Book, Surrey,* edited by John Morris, 1975.

4 *Early Medieval Surrey, Landholding Church and Settlement before 1300,* J. Blair, 1991.

5 Notes by Alfred Goad, (Ass. roll. 7 Edw.1, m/6/2 Im23d No. 3).

6 *Parish Churches,* Cracklow, 1824.

7 *Country Notes,* E.W. Swanton, 1951.
The Hambledon Yew was measured in 1905 by E. W. Swanton, Curator of Haslemere Museum 1897-47. It was 28.5 feet, three feet above ground.

8 *Memories of Hambledon,* Mary Parker, 1989.

9 *Hambledon Parish Magazine,* N. Pollock, January 2000.

10 Ibid.

11 *Memories of Hambledon,* Mary Parker, 1989.

12 Hambledon Village School Log Book, Surrey History Centre, ref: CC/616/3/1.

13 Smith's Charity.
Many Surrey parishes benefitted from the philanthropy of Henry Smith, whose charity was established in the 17th century. Hambledon received a sum yielding 30 shillings to be distributed "to poor housekeepers which do not receive alms of the parish." *Replies to Bishop's Visitations,* Surrey Record Society, Volume XXXIV.

14 The Village Scrapbook.

15 *History of Hambledon Nursery School,* Mary Caröe, 1983.

16 *Memories of Hambledon,* Mary Parker, 1989.

17 *Notice from Poor Law Board,* 3 July 1865.

18 *Memories of Hambledon,* Mary Parker, 1989.

19 Postcard no. 51889 from Francis Frith Collection dated 1904.
The photo of the refurbished almshouses suggests it was mistakenly printed in reverse.

20 Minutes & correspondence held by the Trustees of the Almshouses.

21 *Replies to Bishops Visitations 1725,* Surrey Record Society, Volume XXXIV.

22 *A Topographical Description of Surrey,* Thos. Moule, 1837.

23 The Village Scrapbook.

24 *Witley Lives I*, W. Charles Palmer, 1971.
Footnote: Rosamund Baynes-Powell, Travellers in Eighteenth-century England, Ch. 3, pp. 25-6.

25 *The History of Witley, Milford & Surrounding Area*, Elizabeth Foster, 1999.

26 Cuttings from the Haslemere Herald 1898 in the Village Scrapbook.

27 *Memories of Hambledon*, Mary Parker, 1989.

28 *Birket Foster*, M. Cundall, 1906.

29 The Village Scrapbook.

30 Notes by Sister Cornelia, Bursar at St. Dominic's, 1979.

31 Sale Particulars of Great House Estate, 1906.

32 *Memories of Hambledon*, Mary Parker, 1989.

33 Statutory list.

34 Personal comment, Mrs. Muriel Campbell.

35 Notes by Martin Caröe in the Village Scrapbook.

36 Notes by Martin and Mary Caröe on the history of Vann.

37 Victoria County History, part 23, 1920, Godalming Hundred.

38 *Old West Surrey*, Gertrude Jekyll, 1904.

39 Estate Map 1763.

40 Greater London Record Office (now known as London Metropolitan Archives) ref: DW/PC/6/1836/13.

41 Personal comment, Mr. George Pitt.

42 *The Diaries of Lewis Carroll* edited by Roger Lancelot Green, 1953.

43 *Old West Surrey*, Gertrude Jekyll, 1904.

44 Census Returns 1871.

45 Although described as Hurdle Maker in the Scrapbook, Weald and Downland Museum confirm the photo is of a Hoop Shaver at work.

46 Indenture 7 March 1822 - refers to the Merry Harriers "formerly known by the sign of The Wheatsheaf".
1841 Census - Hare and Hound.

47 *Surrey Archaeological Collections, Volume 62.*

48 Personal comment, Mr. Stephen Dean.

49 *Memories of Hambledon*, Mary Parker, 1989.

50 The Village Scrapbook.

51 *Memories of Hambledon*, Mary Parker, 1989.

52 Personal comment, Roger Milligan, grandson of Frank Milligan.

53 Personal comment, Mr. Stephen Dean.

54 *Hambledon v. Feathercombe 1928-1950*, Winton Dean, 1951.

55 Hambledon Village School Log Book, Surrey History Centre, ref: CC/616/3/1

56 The Village Scrapbook.

List of Illustrations

Hambledon Home Guard